Real Estate Investing:

How To Make Your Riches From Rental Properties and Flipping Houses, And Build Passive Income By Mastering The Property Investment Game

Table of Contents

Introduction

Congratulations on downloading *Real Estate Investing: How To Make Your Riches From Rental Properties and Flipping Houses, And Build Passive Income By Mastering The Property Investment Game* and thank you for doing so. Regardless if you are looking to start investing for the first time or are looking to enhance an existing investment portfolio, real estate is an ideal choice. Ideal, that is, if you choose wisely, but the complex ins and outs of the various types of real estate investment make doing so far from a sure thing.

To help make the process more straight forward, the following chapters will discuss everything you need to know in order to get started with real estate investment successfully starting with the basics including useful investment lingo, how to decide if real estate if real estate is right for you and additional starter tips to help you get started on the right foot. Next, you will learn essentials when it comes to paying for property, finding the ideal property and negotiating the deal when the time comes.

From there you will learn about a wide variety of different real estate investment opportunities including rental property of the traditional and turn key variety as well as the responsibilities that come with being a landlord. You will then learn the ins and out of property flipping including determining when a property is a good deal and building a fix and flip team. Finally, you will learn the basics of property wholesaling and REITs as well.

There are plenty of books on this subject on the market, thanks again for choosing this one! Every effort was made to ensure it is full of as much useful information as possible, please enjoy!

Chapter 1: Why Real Estate?

Real estate is one of the most time-honored investment strategies because, baring the occasional recession, housing prices are almost always going to slowly but surely rise as land is one of the few things that they aren't currently making more of. Investing in real estate means taking on benefits associated with net worth, profitability, cash flow, liquidity, and diversification. Another reason that real estate is the ideal investment choice for the burgeoning investor is that there are so many different real estate investment options to choose from. It doesn't matter what amount you are looking to invest, or what time frame you are hoping to profit in, real estate investment is a viable solution for you.

When it comes to investing in real estate, potential investors have a wide variety of options depending on how hands on they wish to be with their investment. What's more, all types of real estate investment are virtually guaranteed to make at least the industry average 7 percent return on their investment, assuming the market doesn't take one of its infrequent nose dives in the interim. Passive real estate investment can take the form of rental properties that are managed via a property management service, real estate investment trusts which are essential stocks for real estate investment or wholesaling property.

Rental properties are always an attractive option because you know that the property is increasing in value in the long term, while you still make a profit in the short term. Plus, there is nothing like owning an investment that you can physically touch, see and feel. REITs were designed to allow those with relatively limited financial resources to take advantage of the ownership of larger properties including things like shopping centers, office buildings, and hotels. Investors buy into specific REITs and receive a return on their investment equal to the size of the share that they own. Finally, wholesaling property is similar to flipping a property, except without any of the renovation work. In this investment scenario you find a property that has potential, arrange to buy it for a profitable price and then sell that contract to someone who actually follows through on the work, plus several thousand dollars for your time.

Regardless of what type of real estate investment you fancy, you will find that you can make money in four different ways. The first is through a process known as appreciation which is the name given to the natural increase in the value of a given property over time. While this typically amounts to less than 5 percent per year, it is a constant that you don't need to work to generate which means it is, in essence, free money. While appreciation is nice, it is important to never go about making real estate investments based solely on what you believe the appreciation of a property to be, there are always going to be more profitable reasons to consider and if there isn't then the property is a poor value anyway.

Rather than placing an abundance of value on appreciation alone, the best way to go about accurately determining the value of a potential property is to consider the various ways you could make money from it. Investing in property doesn't have to just be places like condominiums or houses, they could also be storage units, laundry mats, car washes and even major investments like large office buildings or hotels. Depending on the type of investment you choose, you may also be able to count on secondary profit streams thanks to pay to use items like vending machines.

Talk the talk
When it comes to being taken seriously in the real estate community and related fields it is important that you understand the jargon and lingo you are likely to encounter on the regular. While you will always want to ask someone to explain a term you haven't heard before as opposed to blindly pressing forward, showing the other person that you know your stuff is still the best-case scenario.

Adverse use: If someone is using a property without the property owner's permission then that property is said to be in the midst of adverse use.

Agreement of sale: The agreement of sale is a document created by a buyer who is interested in purchasing a property that includes the terms they are proposing and any agreement that needs to be outlined between buyer and seller.

Amortization: When the price of a given property is listed as the price that will need to be paid each month that price is said to amortize.

Back to back escrow: Back to back escrow is a situation that occurs when an investor finds themselves working to close a deal on one property while at the same time selling their own property as part of a separate transaction.

Balloon payment: If the payment for a given property is split into multiple payments and the final payment is greater than the average for the other payments then it is referred to as a balloon payment.

Capital gains tax: This is a federal tax that you are required to pay each year based on the appreciation of each property that you own.

Cap rate: Cap rate is the total amount of all profits made from a particular investment property over a specific period of time.

Days on the market: This is the number of the days that a property was listed for sale before it was sold.

Examination of title: When a property is going to be sold, the title that guarantees ownership of it is officially inquired upon and the examination of title results in a list of all of the previous owners going all the way back to when the property was built.

Equity: This is the term given to the total amount the owner of the property can expect to make off of it once all of the relevant expenses accrued in selling it has been taken into account.

Forbearance: Forbearance occurs when a property is in the early stages of foreclosure and the loan lender agrees to put the process on hold and also forgives any late payments the owner of the property currently owes.

Notice of Default: If you own a property and purchased it with a loan, that you are currently not making agreed upon payments on then you will receive a notice of default which lets you know the lender is taking steps to put the property into a state of foreclosure.

Title insurance: This form of insurance protects either the buyer or the seller of a particular piece of property in case the property itself ends up in the middle of a legal dispute.

Walkthrough: This is the final time when the future owner of a property visits the property to make sure everything is on the level before signing the final contract and taking ownership of it.

Is real estate investment right for you?

While real estate is a viable choice for a vast majority of investors, that doesn't mean that it is going to be right for everyone, right now. There are several things you should consider before making the leap as, regardless of the type of real estate investment you choose, it can be a complicated and lengthy endeavor. It is important to take a realistic look at your current situation, and ask yourself the following questions before you make any concrete investing plans.

What are your short term and long term objectives? When creating a plan, you are going to want to start by determining objectives for your investing, which can be broken down into three primary categories, growth, income and safety. If your objective is safety, then you are going to want to focus on keeping the wealth you already have above all else which means that only the bare minimum of risk is allowed. If you are hoping to create a constant stream of income then your objective is going to, unsurprisingly, be income. Finally, if your objective is growth then you are interested in the prospects of the long-term rather than any individual gains that are often based around capital appreciation. When choosing your objectives, you are going to want to be realistic and always factor in your ideal level of risk.

What is your level of risk tolerance?
While every investor's goal is going to be to ultimately end up with more wealth than they started with, the details regarding the specifics are primarily determined by the overall amount of risk that they can tolerate. To understand the concept of risk as it relates to investing, it is important to keep in mind that the various markets that relate to the types of investments in the following chapter are all known to be volatile to one degree or another. The level of volatility a market is prone to is related to the overall amount of movement that the market is going to feel in a given period of time. Investments that are highly volatile are likely to pay out better than those that have a lower volatility, but the chance that you will lose your initial investment is going to be greater as well. Remember, there is no one right way to invest, high volatility or low is primarily a personal preference.

Are you ready to start investing in the long-term?
Current estimates put the amount needed to retire successfully at greater than $500,000. Despite this fact, a vast majority of individuals are not currently saving anywhere near enough to allow them to

support themselves throughout their twilight years. If you are at a point in your life where you are stable enough to consider investing successfully, it may help to first consider what your current income is compared to your monthly bills.

What is your support system like?
While having a support system is always recommended when it comes to making the wisest investments possible, it is especially crucial when you are first getting into real estate investment as there are so many different variables that need to be accounted for in order for the investment to turn out the way you are anticipating. Knowing that you have someone available to run potential deals by can make it easier to invest with confidence so you don't have to worry about secretly losing your shirt with your first deal.

Real estate investment is much more complex than simply purchasing properties and then selling them for a profit which means you will benefit greatly from the insight that a local real estate investment club could provide. These clubs are available in most reasonably sized cities or, barring that, an online forum with an active community could help in much the same way.

Starter Tips

Start an LLC: If you are thinking about investing in real estate, one of the first things that you are going to want to do is to look into the specifics of setting up a Limited Liability Corporation to be in charge of any investments that you make. Doing so will ensure that your personal assets are secure in case something goes wrong down the line somewhere and an accident occurs that is outside the realm that your insurance can pay for. Alternately, if the investment doesn't work out and you are left with debt related to the endeavor, you can simply shutter the LLC and walk away. An LLC can be set up online for as little as $200. While this might seem like an unnecessary step when it comes to real estate investment you are always going to want to try your hardest to plan for the worst while still hoping for the best. Go ahead and take the time to set up your LLC now, if the time comes where you need it, you will be glad you did.

Consider an IRA: IRA is short for Individual Retirement Account and it is a savings account that anyone can set up that offers big tax breaks in return for a strict lock on the funds until you reach retirement age. Much like a 401(k), an IRA lets you invest the money you put into it in a wide variety of ways, including securities and even real estate. There is a limit to how much you can add to them, however, as those under the age of fifty are currently limited to $5,500 per year. Those over fifty are limited to $6,500 per year. You are then allowed to write off your contributions on your taxes.

The limits on IRA investments are pretty broad, you aren't allowed to use it as loan collateral, buy real estate for personal use or lend it to yourself but otherwise, the sky's the limit. While the money you earn on your IRA will be taxed as regular income when you withdrawal it, if you invest in a Roth IRA instead, then your money can grow tax-free. Roth IRAs are funded with post-tax dollars so you will have already paid the required taxes on the funds. Additionally, you are free to leave your money in a Roth IRA for as long as you like, unlike a traditional IRA which requires you to start withdrawing the funds once you hit 59.5 years of age.

Chapter 2: Paying for It

If you are interested in purchasing property as a form of passive income for the smallest amount down possible, you are going to need to put in an extreme amount of time, have a fantastic credit score, be very lucky or some combination of the three. Even then, amazing real estate deals are most certainly the exception, not the rule, and a majority of the properties on the market at any given time are going to require a decent down payment in order to close the deal. With that being said, as long as you are smart about how you make your initial investment you are virtually guaranteed to make a reliable return in the long run.

Consider your circumstances: It is important to consider how stable your career is as a whole, not just your current job. If you are in a risky industry then you need to consider if you feel secure enough in your finances, and the city that you live in, to know that you aren't going to want to move the moment that your current opportunity wraps up. It is important to be honest with yourself during this analysis and to really be sure in your choice as buying a home and then selling it within just a few years is likely going to cost you money, rather than being a profitable investment.

While it's true that you can likely afford to purchase a property for about what you are currently paying in rent, the truth of the matter is that owning a property is about more than that financially. Owning a property means paying homeowner's insurance, HOA fees (if applicable), property taxes and more. Additionally, you can expect your utilities to increase as you will now be on the hook for garbage collection, water, and sewer expenses that you were quite possibly not paying as a renter. What's more, before you go ahead and pull the trigger you are going to want to have a separate fund set aside to pay for in-the-moment home repairs if you don't want to risk dipping into your emergency fund as you know it will come in handy eventually.

Speaking of costs, while in certain circumstances you will be able to qualify for a home mortgage loan through the Federal Housing Administration which means you could get a home for as little as 3.5 percent of the total cost; the majority of home loans that you come across won't be so generous. If you plan on going to a traditional bank for a loan, then you will need to ensure that your credit score is greater than 700 and that your debt coverage ratio is currently greater than 1.25.

Borrowing from a position of strength
In order to ensure you get the best deal on your loan as possible, it is important to know what tools you have at your disposal when it comes to finding the right type of financing. To get started, you are going to want to check your credit report and seek professional help if your score isn't where you want it to be. Unfortunately, a high credit score isn't all that is required these days as the Great Recession has made it much more difficult to finance an investment property than it once was. This means you will naturally start at a disadvantage if you don't have an extensive credit history or lots of previous investment

experience. Difficult is a long way from impossible, however, as long as you approach lenders with the following:

Significant down payment: Currently most traditional lenders are going to require that you have at least 20 percent of the total cost of the investment you are requesting financing for in hand before they will give the go ahead. If you are considering hard money lenders (discussed in detail later in this chapter) then you will likely need 40 percent instead. However, if you can put down an extra 5 percent then you will likely start to see a significant decrease in rates almost immediately. Being able to offer up a larger down payment will also make it more likely that financial institutions will be more forgiving when it comes to overlooking less than perfect credit; this will only take you so far, however.

If you don't have the full 20 percent down payment for the property you are considering, but you qualify for a bank loan in all other respects, then you may want to consider getting two loans rather than just one, just keep in mind that it is going to cut into your profits substantially and it can be more difficult than getting just one mortgage as well. If you do go down this path it is important to plan to pay off one of the mortgages as quickly as possible in order to reduce the overall amount of interest that you ultimately pay.

When approaching a lender, you will want to do so with a well thought out and researched plan that shows a high value to loan ratio as well as a credit score of 740 or higher if you hope to score the best interest rates. If your credit score is lower, the only way you can expect the same rate is by paying more or by paying the same amount and taking a higher interest rate. Regardless, you will want to be able to show that you have the ability to pay all of your expenses for a full six months, plus the expenses of the new property as well if you hope to be considered acceptable.

As a new real estate investor you will likely find that you have better luck trying local banks, as they will already have a legitimate interest in keeping the local economy humming along. They are also likely to have more flexible options more especially tailored for investors in your situation as are mortgage brokers who may also be willing to finance your real estate investment dreams. You won't want to take the first rate they offer you, however, as like in all things related to real estate investment you will find much greater success, and savings, when you do your research. If you are working with a local real estate investment club, which is strongly recommended, they would be the place to start when it comes to the best local lender recommendations.

Finding a lender
If you plan on purchasing not just a single investment rental property but many, then you will likely want to take the extra time to make the effort to find a lender with whom you can build a mutually beneficial long term relationship with. This type of relationship will, in turn, make it easier for the pair of you to come up with a strategy that ensures everyone comes out a winner, not just on this first interaction but during every subsequently one thereafter. You will want to be wary of real estate brokers, however, as they are not

going to offer you the freedom to purchase the ugly duckling properties of your dreams. Remember, the lender is going to directly be responsible for distributing your loans which means it is important to interview them before you full commit to anything. Questions you should ask include things like:

- What is the total number of investors that you are currently working with?
- How many loans would I be able to have active at a single time??
- What types of real estate investments to do you favor?

These questions and other like them will make it easier for you to choose a lender with confidence based on facts, not sales pitches. Remember, if you don't like something about an individual that's completely fine, as long as you act accordingly and move on to keep from wasting everyone's time in both the short and the long run. If you can't seem to find the lender that's right for you, it is important to not despair and to instead keep at it. If you are looking to put down as little up front as you possibly can, title loans, credit cards or equity loans based on other property that you own are always an option, though they should be exercised with caution.

Lender alternatives

P2P: Over the past few years a number of peer-to-peer (P2P) real estate investment websites have popped up offering both short term and long term loan options for those interested in buying and fixing up a property without the cash on hand to pay for it themselves.

Investing in these types of loans is often referred to as Trust Deed investing which means the investor is a private source of capital which is then loaned to the borrower. This investment is secured by a Trust Deed, hence the name and is the same regardless of which P2P lending platform you decide to use.

P2P real estate loans often have a number of benefits when it compared with more traditional bank loans, the first of which is that they are much easier for those seeking loans to qualify for. They are also often much less rigid in terms of guidelines than traditional loans and often go through in a matter of hours, not weeks or months. They are also ideal for those looking to generate passive income streams because they don't require the investment of the full price of the property as with real world transactions. Instead, investors are able to invest the amount they are comfortable with and a clear idea of the repayment terms they can expect.

As with any other type of real estate investment, it is important to have a clear idea of the risks and benefits associated with the property in question. To that end, it is important to have a basic understanding of what the After Repair Value (ARV) of any property you are looking at is going to be. ARV can be thought of as the amount the property is going to be worth once the project is fully finished. This amount needs to be enough to cover the proposed costs of purchasing the property as well as renovations with enough left over to turn a profit for the person who is working on the property.

Owner financing: Depending on how you plan on making a profit from the property, you may find that asking the seller for owner financing can be a reliable way to ensure that you don't need to worry about a loan at all, as long as you can get rid of the property before the inspection window closes and you actually need to come up with the money. Prior to 2009, practically anyone could get an investment property loan as long as they were able to actually walk into a bank and ask about receiving one. As such, those who couldn't a loan via traditional means was naturally mistrusted which meant asking about owner financing was a no go.

Things are different these days, however, as it is public knowledge that banks are more skittish when it comes to giving out loans and sellers are more willing to just get things done regardless of how the deal gets made. In fact, currently, more than 30 percent of all sellers are willing to consider owner financing for the right buyer which means you are going to need to have everything prepared from the previous chapter in order to show that you are a reliable investment. Once you do obtain owner financing you will then sign a promissory note saying when you will pay back the loan in full, what your monthly payments are going to be, when these payments start and what the interest rate is like.

If you have access to a contractor who can get materials on credit, then it is possible that you could sell the owners on the idea of selling you the house with the promise to pay them in full once it is renovated and resold for more than it is going for now. This will obviously not be feasible in all situations, but for owners who are already fairly well off who are not selling for emergency reasons this can be thought of as a type of investment and if you can prove them numbers you might be on to something.

Chapter 3: Finding Property Basics

It doesn't matter what type of real estate investment you are looking forward to investing in, you won't be able to realistically move forward if you aren't able to find a property that will end up putting enough money in your pocket to be worth all the hard work. Luckily, you won't be without options when it comes to finding the best properties for the cheapest possible price.

Find the right area
In order to be successful when you look for properties to purchase it is vital that you take the time to research your target areas ahead of time to prevent yourself from wasting time looking at details of properties that aren't going to work out in the long-term and also to ensure that when you find a good deal you are aware of what you have on your hands and can plan accordingly. Finally, this research is important when it comes to knowing if the price a seller is asking for is reasonable or completely off base.

In order to find the right area to focus on you are going to want to choose one that has properties of varying price ranges and a property tax rate that is low for the area. Checking into the property tax rate is a crucial step in the process because properties that are only a few streets from one another could have wildly different tax rates.

It is important to visit any areas you are considering in person and talk to the locals to make sure there isn't anything hiding just under the surface that you are missing. You can learn more about most neighborhoods by spending 15 minutes in them in person than you can reading about them for an hour or more online. You will want to get a feel for the neighborhood and its charms as well as the people who call it home. The best people to talk to are often renters as those who own a property in an area are more likely to make excuses for it. You should also check with the local police station for current crime statistics.

You will also want to consider the main attractions around the neighborhoods that you are considering and how they would appeal to your primary renting audience. Are you looking for someplace a family might want to call home? Then check out the schools in the area and make finding property near the best ones a priority. On the contrary, maybe the nightlife potential is more of a factor, whatever it is, doing your homework means more than simply knowing everything there is to know about the home in question.

Regardless of your target audience, it is always beneficial to look at properties that are close to a local business district and also to always keep abreast of any major changes coming to the area such as companies moving into or out of town. If a big company is coming in then they are likely going to be bringing new employees with them while if the company is on its way out then you know to avoid the area in case it can't recover from the loss.

Finding Properties through Online Listings

The most basic and freest option that you have when you're looking for a good real estate to purchase is no longer a newspaper. Instead, it's the internet. In addition to Zillow and the MLS database, some other sites that will be able to provide you with quality online listings include the following:

LoopNet.com: Unlike Zillow, LoopNet is able to provide its users with exclusively commercial real estate opportunities. To this end, there are advantages to using LoopNet that you won't find elsewhere. These include being able to compare sale prices within a given locale, as well as look at a property's history as well as provide you with information regarding purchase and selling trends.

Auction.com: If you're looking for a property that you could possibly acquire for cheaper than its market value and you have a knack for the foreclosure or short sale market, then using Auction.com should be a no-brainer. With Auction.com, you don't have to travel to a physical location in order to partake in the auction process if you don't want to. You're able to participate in auctions online, as well as be offered the ability to travel to locations where an auction is taking place. This site also keeps track of auctions in various parts of the nation and updates this information on their website in the form of a calendar.

Craigslist: Craigslist? Really? While Craigslist might get a bad rep, the reality is that it can be a great place to find homes that are being sold by owners and people who do not desire to work with a Realtors. Craigslist can also be a great starting point for when you're looking to negotiate with people and get them to lower their prices. This is especially true if they're not working with a Realtors, or they feel as if their property is too rundown to be considered profitable by a real estate agent.

MLS

The multiple listing service (MLS) is an excellent place to look for current listings as it contains a regularly updated list of all of the properties on the market in the country that are being sold by licensed realtors. As anyone is free to look at the current list, you can expect the best deals to go quite quickly which means if you are going to go this route you are going to want to check it around 5 am EST and again before you go to bed in order to ensure you don't miss out on the best deals.

Even with this level of diligence, you should still be prepared for some stiff competition, however, as there are as many great deals on the site as there are people who are looking to take advantage of them. Generally speaking, you can plan on finding the best deals first thing Monday and Friday morning as these will be the days that include the least competition. This is because working in real estate allows for an extremely flexible schedule which many people use as an excuse to take a weekend that starts early or ends late. Thus, if you make the extra effort on these days you can reap the rewards.

Know what you are looking for: When looking through the MLS listings, the most important thing to keep an eye out for are properties that have been on the market once and are now back for a repeat performance. What this means is that the original deal for the property fell through which also means the owner is far more likely to be willing to negotiate than would otherwise be the case. These types of sellers are often just looking to be done with the entire process which means you can often find a great deal if you are the first person to show up with cash in hand or preapproved for a loan.

Finally, MLS is useful because sometimes you will simply get lucky. There are thousands of new MLS listings every day which means if you keep it up you are virtually guaranteed to stumble across a good deal eventually. Sometimes it might be in the form of a short sale that you see just as it is listed or you might find a property that is listed low expressly to be sold quickly. This is why it is worth checking each and every day, you never know what might be waiting on the next page.

Sellers who are motivated

If you are really looking to pick up properties on the cheap, then you may want to avoid MLS completely by looking for properties that have not yet made it to that part of the process. This means looking for sellers who you have reason to believe are especially motivated and doing something that benefits both parties. The goal is to find sellers who have yet to reach out to a real estate agent, leaving you far more in control than may otherwise be the case. Once a seller goes ahead and hires a real estate agent the possibility of getting the best possible deal goes out the window which is why reaching out to those who have not yet thought about selling their home such an effective tactic.

Where to find them: The first thing you need in order for this process to be successful is, unsurprisingly, to find the type of homeowners who would be classified as motivated sellers which are people who are currently in urgent need of a serious influx of cash for to the point that their debts are already in collections and the fact that someone might come and take their home may have already occurred to them. The easiest way to find a list of people in this situation is to go online and find a company that will sell you a list of debtors in your area. This should only take a few minutes in even a small city and will likely set you back between $200 and $300.

After you have this list the next step is to head to the local clerk of the court to cross check the names you have with a list of property owners to see who on your list warrants a closer look. Once you have finished narrowing down your list, the next thing you will want to do is generate a form letter to mail to your motivated sellers. The basics of your letter should include lip service towards their plight as well as a concise explanation of how you can help them and the fact that you have access to enough money to clear their debt completely. You will want to stop short of making an offer at the moment, however, as this is better done in person where you can get a clear measure of the state the motivated seller is in. You will finish the letter with your contact details and then let the deals come to you.

While not every person you send a letter to will contact you, it will only take a small number of interested parties to keep you busy for a year or more. Generally speaking, you can expect a direct mailing campaign targeted in this way to see a roughly 3 percent response which means that for every 100 letters you send out 3 people will be in touch. Thus, for a minimal monetary and time investment, you can virtually guarantee a steady supply of sellers who are interested in talking to you without having to deal with competition in any shape or form. What's more, the properties you purchase in this way are virtually guaranteed to be available for less than market value.

Courthouse auction: While not available everywhere, in many states, you will find that if a lean holder forecloses on a property the last step is for the property to be auctioned off. While these types of auctions rarely take place at the actual courthouse these days, they remain an excellent way to purchase property for pennies on the dollar, though the amount of information you have on the property in question is going to vary dramatically. Details for these types of auctions can be found in the local paper or on the local municipality website.

Bidding on these properties starts at whatever the lienholder is owed so the bidding can be pretty fierce in some instances and still come out to far less than what the property is actually worth. As the information available is going to vary dramatically between auctions, it is important to try and track down as much information about each property as possible as a means of limiting potential risk. Greater rewards come with greater risk, however, and if you are lucky you could easily end up with a property that far exceeds what your budget would otherwise be. It shouldn't be surprising that you need to have cash on hand or a preapproved loan ready to go for these types of auctions as there is no waiting no matter what.

Chapter 4: Negotiating a Deal

The golden rule in real estate is that everything is negotiable, and this is true, up to a point. When you are buying your first real estate investment property you are going to naturally want to get the best deal that you can to maximize your future profits, this doesn't mean you need to haggle over ever last red cent, however, and sometimes knowing when to stop is as important as knowing when to go full bore.

The best way to learn the limits starts with knowing the area surrounding the property as thoroughly as possible, down to the neighborhood and street if possible. First things first, if there are more homes for sale in the area than the local average then this means you are lucky enough to find yourself in a buyer's market. This means you are going to be able to make more demands and even take an extra 10 percent off any offers that you make. If the alternative is true then you are looking at a seller's market which means that you are going to be lucky to pay the asking price and might need to make a few more concessions than you otherwise would.

With so many home listings available online, it can be easy to see the logic in trying to save some extra money by not using a real estate agent during your real estate investment endeavors. It is more difficult than you might expect to get a property successfully from offer to close, however, and there is a lot you can learn from a good real estate agent that makes them worthwhile your first few times out at least. A good agent will also have negotiation experience and insider details about the market that can pull a successful deal together from almost nothing. What's more, as the buyer, you won't be paying for the agent, that will be covered in a commission paid by the seller. When it does come time to try the process yourself, however, consider the following tips to help you start off on the right foot.

Three part process: All successful negotiation can be broken up into three parts, process, behavior, and substance. Process is the way in which you approach a given negotiation, and a confident process can do wonders when it comes to effective negotiations. Substance can be thought of as the details at the heart of the negotiation, and your process should ensure the substance goes in your favor as well. Finally, you can think of the interaction between you and the other party as the behavior of the negotiation.

Do it face to face: When it comes to submitting an offer, you are going to always want to meet with the other party directly if possible. Assuming the market is in your favor, then you are going to have most of the power going into the negotiation and the best way to capitalize on that power is to meet the other person face to face. Alternatively, if the market is currently in the other party's favor you are going to want to negotiate via email instead as this will balance out the power disparity somewhat. When meeting a new seller it is important to listen to the way they say things as well as what is being said. Tonality is actually a combination of two things, volume, and pace. To ensure you get off to a good start with a potential seller you will want to match them on both accounts. This means you are going to want to speak quietly to reserved customers and be brash with those who tend to only use their outdoor voices. A disconnect in either way will make them feel uncomfortable and can potentially cost you the sale as a result.

When you do actually submit your offer, however, you are going to want to do so and then remain completely silent, no matter how long it takes. If the other party also appears to be dead set on not saying anything either, after 90 seconds you can repeat your offer once more. This will limit the other party significantly in terms of how they can proceed, firmly establishing your power in the negotiation even more.

Another reason that you will want to hold the negotiations in person as long as the conditions are favorable is that you can learn a lot about the other person via their body language. If the other submits a counteroffer while using open body language then this means they are more willing to reach a consensus with you. Closed body language, meanwhile indicates that they are not pleased with your original offer and they are less willing to come to an agreement as a result. If they come back with timid body language, however, then this means you likely have them over a barrel and can remain firm.

You are also going to want to make a point of using open body language as well. A defensive, closed body posture automatically tells those around you that you are tense, nervous and unwilling to come to a mutually beneficial agreement. This isn't a secret science either, these are common body language cues that you can bet money on that the seller can read as well, even if this is just subconsciously.

What's worse, once they are aware of them, most sellers will start mimicking them, and their related behaviors as well. Closed body posture gives them the signal that there's something to worry about and they'll fell ill at ease and much more resistant to persuasion. The fix, luckily, is quite simple. If you concerned you may be displaying a defensive body posture, all you need to do is sit up straight so that your spine is aligned, and your shoulders are squared. At the same time, you are going to want to breathe deeply, place your hands on your legs, with your palms up. While this isn't a natural position, it is an important part of the overall whole.

Opening up your posture in this way will also serve to improve your mental state by decreasing the amount of the hormone cortisol that your body produces. Cortisol is responsible for stress levels so in this case acting and outwardly appearing to be calm and collected will make you feel this way as well, relaxing your potential customers in the process.

Consider the market: It is also important to keep the current state of the market in mind as well as this will help set the stage for the entire negotiation. If the market is currently favorable to buyers then you will be able to make additional demands without worrying about the seller backing out. What's even better, you can typically take at least 10 percent off your asking price without losing out. You can even ask the seller to pay the closing costs. On the other hand, if it is currently a seller's market then you will need to be ready to make concessions where appropriate, pay the asking price, and pay the closing costs.

Make the right first impression: Studies show that, statistically speaking, the person who enters the negotiation space with less baggage is going to start off the negation from a greater place of power. Entering the negotiation space should be a streamlined process that makes you look as though you are as ready to get down to business as quickly as possible. Once you start off on the right foot, seize the advantage that it creates with the proper business handshake and a seat that is at a 45-degree angle from the other party to show you are interested in collaborating for everyone's benefit.

Consider your opposition: When it comes to taking stock of the other party in the negotiation, the first thing you are going to want to do is to be aware of the more obvious verbal cues such as erratic gestures, shifty eyes, murmuring, sweating, shaking or excessive blinking are all signs that things are not on the level. While few professional negotiators go about things in such an obvious fashion, you never know what might slip through subconsciously which is why it pays to always keep an eye on the little things.

Other important body language to be on the lookout for includes anything that generates a physical barrier. Common examples of this are crossed arms or holding documents or other props in hand and pressed tightly to the chest. These are all signs that the other person is not receptive to what the other person is saying. In fact, one study looked at more than 2,000 negotiations take place and none of them ended in success if one member never uncrossed their arms.

Regardless of what you find when inspecting the other party, it is important to file it away and use it as a baseline when it comes to determining what affect, if any, your persuasive skills are having. If you instead find the other party to be clearly and obviously ill-prepared this is likely to be a trick. Be on your guard and you are more likely to come out on top regardless of the specifics of the interaction.

Hold eye contact: When it comes to negotiating effectively it is important to maintain eye contact to convey that you trust the other party and are, in turn, trustworthy yourself. You should also make a concentrated effort to increase the amount of eye contact that you are using while you are speaking and use slightly less than normal while the other person is speaking to show that you are in the dominant position and you know it. It is important to break it off before things get too tense, however, as you don't want to take things all the way to aggressive territory.

Pupil constriction and squinting can mean the person is bothered by what they are seeing. A long exhale can mean that the person is under extreme emotional distress. As it is common knowledge that not looking another person in the eyes is a sign of lying, those who lie will often try to overcompensate for this fact which is a great way to determine if they are actually lying after all.

The average amount of eye contact sits at between 7 and 10 seconds in most cultures, during the average conversation, as a sign that both parties are active and committed to the conversation. If the person you are speaking with is holding your gaze in such a way that it makes you want to squirm, resist the urge and instead consider what about the conversation is making them act in such a strange way.

When looking for excessive eye contact, it is also important to pay attention to what the other person's eyebrows are doing as well. Raised eyebrows are typically a sign of discomfort. In fact, raised eyebrows are generally associated with fear, worry or surprise, none of which signal a relaxing conversation with a friend. As such, if you see this automatic response, and it occurs around a topic you wouldn't expect, then you may need to dig a little deeper to determine what exactly is going on.

Play the odds: Statistically speaking, even if it is your first time negotiating a contract, one hundred percent failure is practically impossible to achieve. To that end, if you make a point of running towards instances where you can lowball a seller, you will eventually find one that works out in your favor, guaranteed. While it might take more effort than you would hope for, once you get an extremely good deal once then you will be able to hold onto that memory and it will make it dramatically more likely you will see a second sooner than later. Eventually, you will find that the percentage of times you find it easy to play hard ball during negotiations has swung back around to your favor and from there it will be a simple matter of making it a habit with every property you look at moving forward.

Practice empathy: Empathy needs to become your best friend when you want to negotiate with a seller successfully. Many people think that they have the whole empathy thing down, but any time they are confronted with a situation where they could feel for the other person, they end up failing. People all live different lives, have different troubles, and react differently to the things that go on in their lives. Being able to put yourself in their shoes and understand what is going on can be a big challenge, especially when we are so caught up in our own personal lives. Doing so will ultimately make it easier for you to see the chinks in their armor and find the secret to ensuring the negotiations end up in your favor.

If you are struggling with the whole idea of empathy, it may be time to start working on it a bit more. Start with one person. Make it your goal for the week to think the way that this particular person would in each situation. Instead of acting the way that you would or think that you would react the way that you think they would. This can help you to get a deeper understanding of what is going on with those around you.

Chapter 5: Rental Property Basics

If you are looking for something a little bit more substantial, then you may be interested in a duplex or a small apartment complex with around 6 units or less. Properties with multiple tenants are nice because much more needs to go wrong overall before you suddenly find yourself in a situation where you are not receiving enough to cover the costs of the property in a given month. The biggest concern for these types of properties is the type of tenants who call them home to start as they are going to be one of the most influential factors when it comes to finding future tenants. Depending on the size of the property in question you may even be able to trade property management services in exchange for free board and then you would be able to count on someone being on the premises at all times.

When it comes to renting out a single-family home, you will often find that the easiest way to go about doing so is by using what is known as a turnkey rental property company. So called because the property is completely ready for a renter to move into on purchase, these types of properties require little from you except the initial payment as the company is then in charge of the property management and virtually everything else. As such, it is extremely important that you do your research in this instance otherwise you can easily end up in a bad situation that you are contractually required to follow through on. Additionally, it is extremely important that no matter what you are told you always visit the property in person before committing to everything. Remember, an ounce of prevention is worth a pound of cure.

Rental property considerations: Assuming you plan to do so from the beginning, using a property management company to manage your rental properties creates a passive income opportunity from the moment you close on the property in question. As such, it is important to research property management companies in the area you are planning on purchasing property in to see what their requirements and costs are. Typically, it is difficult to find a property management company for a single, single family home which means a small duplex or fourplex might be the way to go. Alternatively, condominiums are also great for first time investors as they are more likely to attract stable individuals and they come with a built-in property manager as well.

Condominiums are a great choice for a first passive income rental property for several reasons. First, you know there will always be someone on site and you don't even need to worry about paying additional fees for a property manager. Additionally, the types of renters that are looking for condos are typically upwardly mobile professionals which means you will rarely. need to worry about payments being spotty or being made late.

On the other hand, a duplex requires less work than an apartment complex, but more than a condo and it will be important to screen potential renters thoroughly to ensure you don't get stuck paying for the property while dealing with getting someone evicted. Finally, a small apartment complex is nice because you don't need to worry about paying your bills as long as a simple majority of tenants can pay their rent on time. As an added bonus, if you can find a reliable person to be your on premises representation then you might not even need to hire a property management company.

Getting started

Do your homework: Once you have decided on the type of rental property that you are interested in purchasing, the first thing you are going to want to do is to narrow down your search to neighborhoods that are going to attract the interest of the types of tenants you are looking for. If you are planning on purchasing a single-family home, then that means you are going to want to consider areas that have amenities that families are looking for which means things like parks or schools. Meanwhile, if your target renter is instead younger and single then you are going to want to consider local nightlife possibilities.

Regardless of who your target renter might be you are always going to want to consider what the employment options are like in the area, and not just on a superficial level either. Digging deeper to find out if any major companies are planning to move into, or out of, specific areas can often give you a heads up on where the rental market in a specific area is going to be like six months or more down the line.

Do the math: When you come across a property that you are interested in learning more about, the first thing that you will want to do is to run the numbers and ensure that it will work out to be worth your time in the long run. If you aren't sure what you might be able to get for a specific property each month in rent the easiest way to come up with a ballpark number is to simply look at other rental properties in the area and see what the rent is like. With a ballpark number in mind, you can then tweak your personal number based on the property in question and anything that is unique about it.

Rental property tips
Fix it up to a point: After you have found a property in an area that you like for an amount that you can afford to actually pull the trigger on, the next thing you are going to want to do is to get it ready to put on the market. When it comes to getting their first rental property ready for actual renters, it is common for new property owners to go overboard and make the property as impeccable as possible. While going all out is something that your tenants will appreciate, it isn't something that they are willing to pay extra for, however, which is why you are going to want to approach the renovations with a critical eye.

This doesn't mean that you want to leave things in a dank, dangerous or dingy fashion, but it does mean that you don't need to worry about fixing up every nook and cranny. As long as you replace the kitchen cabinets and counters and give the bathroom a bit of a makeover, lots of smaller issues will be accepted by tenants without so much as a peep. Additionally, if your budget is tight, a high likelihood if this is your first rental property, then you can easily hold off on replacing long-term systems until they give out as you are going to be responsible for the repairs or replacements regardless. Finally, when it comes to painting the property you are going to want to stick with something besides white that will work with numerous color palates.

Charge the right amount for rent: Once you find a property that appears as though it meets your needs, the next thing you are going to want to do is to run the potential numbers to ensure it is actually going to be worth it for you to move forward. This means you are going to want to look into the current rental prices for other, similar properties in the area so you can get a basic idea of what's reasonable before factoring in the things that make the property you are looking into unique and adjusting accordingly. Once you have a number in mind, all you need to do is add up the cost that you will pay for insurance, loan payment, property management fees, and taxes and subtract that result from the likely rent amount.

Whatever is leftover is what you as the property owner are going to be entitled to, if it seems like a reasonable number to you then you can go ahead with the property. You will also need to factor in another 10 percent of the total costs to account for any vacancies or missed payments that you can expect to experience now and then. Additionally, you can plan on the property appreciating 3 percent each year, which should be enough to pay for some of the existing fees.

Advertising
Once you have actually finished with a property and it is ready to rent out, the first thing to do is get the word out about it which means taking lots of pictures both inside and out. While you certainly want to show the property in the best light, it is important to not

employ any intentionally misleading tactics to make things look better than they are. Doing so will certainly bring in more people but the contrast between the fiction you created and the reality of the property may be enough to turn them off, even if they would have been alright with the flaw in the first place.

When creating online profiles for your rental, it is important to list all the best features of the property in a way that is both clear and succinct. Renters are used to having to wade through piles of useless information to get the details they are looking for so by putting them up front you are sure to grab their attention. When creating your profiles be sure to include things like relation to local schools, public transit options, relation to important local areas, swimming pool, air conditioning, laundry room and anything else that sets the property apart including major renovations you have completed.

Additionally, you will need to clearly present the size of the entire lot as well as the size of the livable space and the policies on things like smoking, deposits, and pets. If time is of the essence and you are looking to get a tenant in the property as quickly as possible without sacrificing long-term profits by simply dropping the rent is to include rent or utilities for a limited time, reduce the amount of deposit that is required or cut the first month's rent by a small portion. While this will certainly cut into your short-term profits, it may be a better solution than letting the property sent empty for a prolonged period of time.

Renting out the property as quickly as possible also means casting as wide of a net as possible which means taking to social media and asking all of your friends to help spread the word as well. Statistically speaking, everyone under the age of 30 is only two degrees of separation removed from someone who is currently looking for or will soon be looking for a new place to live which means a little social media traction is likely all it would take to start seeing real results. Beyond going viral you will not want to underestimate the effectiveness of putting a for rent sign in the front yard which is still how roughly 25 percent of renters found their current residence. You will also want to seek out exclusively regional or local rental services and even the local newspaper can prove a surprisingly effective choice when it comes to attracting new tenants.

A slightly pricier option, though one that is ideal for high quality or niche properties, is to utilize a real estate professional who specializes in the type of property you are looking to rent. If your first rental property is likely to just be the first of many then creating a long-term relationship with someone in this field could lead to years of mutually beneficial business while saving your hundreds of hours in the long-term.

Regardless of your ideal rental plans, it is important to never settle for a subpar tenant (like those discussed in chapter 7) just to prevent the property from sitting empty for a month or two. While it can hurt to have to pay the upkeep on the property while waving goodbye to early profits, the headaches that come along with trying to force out a poor tenant are not something you want to have to deal with if you can possibly avoid it. On the contrary, a good tenant is literally worth their weight in gold and will make it easy for you to ensure your rental property becomes a true passive income stream.

Screening tenants
Once word has gotten out about your new property, it will be time to ensure you find the best possible tenants to keep it looking as nice as is reasonably possible. The screening policy that will be best for you is going to vary from landlord to landlord based on personal preferences, as well as the overall amount of risk you are comfortable dealing with. The most important factor, however, is that you have your specifics in mind and stick to your guns no matter what. As a general rule, however, you should consider the following for your first tenants:

- No previous history of evictions
- Positive references from the previous landlord and current employer
- An acceptable background check which often includes a criminal history clear of misdemeanors and felonies for the previous seven years
- A sum total household income that is three times the total rent when all tenants' income is combined

While you are clearly free to add any additional specifics you might like, you should find that this level of specificity is enough to weed out the types of tenants that are going to cause you problems. When it comes to screening potential renters the process should start with the prescreening which takes place when the potential tenant first sees the property. You should ask them if they meet the requirements that you are going to be looking. This will cut out the honest folks who don't want to waste your time. You should not disqualify them out of hand, however, as an honest tenant is a valuable asset and you should look more closely at the specifics of their situation.

Those who make it through the prescreening phase should then receive an application which will ask for things like relevant personal details, employment information, social security number, and references. If you pull an application from the internet take care to make sure it includes a waiver saying you are allowed to run a background check and a credit check on the applicant for the purpose of determining their eligibility to rent the property.

Background checks can be provided by third-party companies or by the state directly, though specifics will vary by location. You can obtain a credit report on an individual directly from one of the three credit bureaus Equifax, Experian and TransUnion, and this request can be made online. Generally speaking, you should aim for a renter with a credit score of 600 minimum, though something higher might be warranted depending on what you have set the desired rent at.

If you still don't feel quite right about a given applicant after running the checks, this is when you would want to go ahead and call any proffered references, after all, that's what they are there for.

When you do make the call you are allowed to ask about anything that is relevant to your decision, as long as it is within reason. If you end up not liking a particular potential tenant then it is legally required that you send them a letter explaining why they were not selected. This is known as a letter of adverse action and it should state what information you gathered and how it affected your decision. You are required to provide this letter within 60 days to anyone whose application you deny.

Chapter 6: Turnkey Rental Properties

A turnkey property is any property that can be purchased with the promise of generating cash flow as quickly as possible, in some cases already with renters attached. There are two primary ways of going about finding a turnkey property to purchase, the first provides greater returns, and the second provides the simplest buying experience possible. First of all, if you are interested in making as much off of a property as possible, your best bet is to find a property that is ready rent out immediately, do the leg work of finding a tenant and then find a property management company who will take you on as a client. Once you have put all of the pieces together yourself, you will find that you manage to retain about 90 percent of the total rental price each month.

Alternatively, you can go through a turnkey property company that specializes in working with investors just like you. In this case, you would only need to choose the company you are interested in working with, pay them for a property and then wait for the profits to roll in. In most instances, you can expect to both pay more for the property up front and also see a smaller return from each month's rent when going this route. On the other hand, in most cases when you purchase a turnkey property from a turnkey company you can expect to start making money back on your investment the very next month.

As you will be planning to hire a professional management company anyway, it is important to understand that the biggest difference between the two is typically going to be how involved you want to be in the process of investment property ownership. While a property management company means you won't have to deal with the property on the regular, issues may arise from time to time that will still require your attention. If you choose to go with a turnkey company the only time you will have to think about your property is when you receive a monthly check in the mail for your part of the profits.

The location that you plan on purchasing a turnkey rental property in will also likely play a part in whether or not you choose to go with a turnkey rental property company over a choose your own property type of approach. Turnkey rental properties are becoming an increasingly popular investment opportunity for those who live in areas where land is scarce, simply because it allows them to easily invest in areas where the property is much more affordable than anything they could ever hope to find locally. Investors looking to set up this type of investment opportunity would naturally gravitate towards a turnkey rental property company simply because it would allow them to know that their property is going to be in good hands even when they are all the way across the country, if not the world.

Choosing a turnkey property company
While the benefit of finding a turnkey property company is that you have to do little more than sit back and wait for the profits to start rolling in, that doesn't mean that is all you ever have to do from day one. Before you reach the point of passive income you are going to want to ensure that you have done plenty

of research to ensure that you are going to be ready for everything that the process of finding the right turnkey rental real estate company is going to throw at you.

Separate the wheat from the chaff: When it comes to finding the right turnkey rental real estate company for you, the first thing you are going to want to do is to immediately disqualify any company that doesn't have a physical address and does all of their business through the internet. While the online world has been able to automate many real estate based functions when it comes to a turnkey rental investment you are going to want to know there is some place that you can physically take your complaints to if things do not initially go as planned.

The truth of the matter is that a real, viable turnkey rental property company is going to have a website that is virtually indistinguishable from a fake simply because both are going to show nothing but great looking homes and make promises that you as an investor want to hear. These companies can then easily cash quite a few checks before anyone catches on to the scam and, what's worse, can be in the wind and ready to do it again before anyone even gets close to finding them. Do your rental property investment a favor and treat it with caution, the turnkey rental property company you pick is going to be in charge of your investment completely, treat the choice with the importance it deserves.

Weed out the newer companies: After you have made a point of avoiding any company without a physical location, the next thing that you will need to do is to cross from your list any company that has been in business for less than a decade. The turnkey rental property business is extremely competitive and it takes quite some time to master the intricacies of a particular area; what this means is that if you go with a new turnkey rental property company then you are essentially paying them to learn with your money. Avoid the learning curve entirely, pick a company that is clearly going to know what it is doing because it has been doing it for more than a decade.

The best way to find these types of companies is to look into personal recommendations from someone that you know and trust. Barring a local recommendation, you are going to want to look into the recommendations left by other users online. While a single review, positive or negative, shouldn't sway you one way or another, what you are going to be interested in tracking down are patterns that appear over time concerning the particular turnkey rental property company.

Start with the basics: With the worst of the worst accounted for, the next thing you will need to do is make sure the remaining companies you are looking at have a number of basic things in any reviews you read. For starters, it is important that the company has a long history of success, 10 years minimum. Anything less than this means they might still be working the kinks out of their business or still learning the ropes and you don't want them learning with your money. You will also want to pay special attention to reviews that discuss details that relate to the management or repairs and renovations. Above all, you want to get the feeling that they really are focused on their investors. Verifying this data through a third party is also encouraged.

Reach out to the companies you like the most: Assuming this process has whittled down your list to just a handful of potential candidates, the next thing you are going to want to do is to reach out to each of the companies you are considering in person to see what they are like to deal with. This means you are going to want to track down a phone number, not an email address as you want to know you can call someone directly if an emergency occurs. The more ways a company provides you to get in touch with them, the more likely they are to truly care about receiving customer feedback. Long story short, if any of the companies still on your list only offer email communication then you are going to want to cross them off right away.

When you do reach out to these companies it is important that you wait to see how long it takes them to get back to you and avoid them in the future if it takes them more than 24 hours to return your initial call. After all, if it is clear they don't care about your business right from the start, consider how much worse things are going to be once they already have you under contract. Alternately, they could simply be too busy or too poorly managed to call you back in a timely fashion but these are all signs that you will be better off with another company instead.

Professionalism: Once you have narrowed your list down even more, you will then want to consider how professional the representative you speak with is as this is indicative of the overall level of professionalism of the company as a whole. As someone who is likely not even in the same state as the property you are considering, it is extremely important that you can trust the company you are leaving your investment too and their level of professionalism is a good indication of such.

Likewise, it is important that you can get in touch directly with the person who is managing your property at all times and also that they do more than pay you lip service and go about their day. This means you are going to want to ensure they are never to busy to speak with you or go over some detail of the process, no matter how relatively minor. You should make it a point to come up with excuses to talk to this person multiple times before you sign anything to ensure you have a good measure of what they are really like.

Another important aspect of the company to consider is the level of knowledge the people you speak with have when it comes to their local market as well as the wider market as a whole. By this point in the process, you should already know everything about the area you are considering purchasing property in so it should be relatively straightforward to test their knowledge on the area. Don't be afraid to press them on apparent discrepancies either, they may have more up to date information than you do, after all, and you may end up learning something as well.

Additionally, when you reach out to these companies you should be able to rely on more than their word and your own observations, they should be able to point you towards satisfied customers who can vouch for their level of quality. If you come across a company that is unable to provide you with valid references then you may need to consider why this might be the case. You should also reach out to references with different numbers of rental properties to ensure that no one is getting superior service unduly or based on personal biases.

One area that should be of particular interest is the level of support the company provides after the sale has already been completed. Even if the company has been quite attentive to you so far, having the viewpoint of a person who has already been through the process is vital to ensure that nothing is going to change once the paperwork is signed. Additionally, other investors will be the ones to know if the turnkey company you are dealing with outsources the actual property management duties which means you may need to look into them separately as well.

It is especially important to be aware of this final scenario as this type of setup is not recommended as it often leads to a variety of additional issues before the deal can be closed successfully. If you do decide to go down this route then then it is vital that you do the leg work required to ensure the property management is on the level to avoid needless hassle when you are so close to success.

Consider the pricing: While initially there are any number of reasons why you may be tempted to go after a turnkey property that is priced more competitively than its competition. It is important to avoid this impulse, however, as it will likely end up costing you more in the long-term than you might expect. The research you have done on the area should give you a good idea of what the property in question should go for, and you can bet the company you are looking at knows this as well. As turnkey properties are expected to be at or above market value, the only logical reason this would not be the case then is if something not entirely above board is going on. Whatever it is, the goal of this type of real estate investment is to be as passive as possible and this is a red flag that your experience is going to be anything but straightforward.

Chapter 7: Fulfilling the Role of Landlord

Tenant Types to Avoid

In a perfect world, you, as the landlord, could expect to provide a quality service and, in turn, be treated with respect by a tenant who is eager to make the process as simple for everyone involved as possible. This is rarely the case, however, and if you aren't careful you can find yourself dealing with a tenant that costs you time as well as money. While you will eventually develop a quality screening process that works for you, for now, you will likely find it helpful to keep an eye out for the following types of tenants, so you can avoid them at all costs.

The destructive tenant: There is no type of tenant worse for your newly minted rental property than the destructive tenant. Whether they have a destructive child or pet that they have no control over, remodel a portion of the property to better suit their needs, or are simply not respectful to the property, this type of tenant is likely to cause extreme damage to your property and then try and do their best to get you to pay for it.

Luckily, it is often possible to pick out a destructive tenant when they come to look at the property, as long as you think to look for the signs. First, you are going to want to be sure to meet them by their vehicle as its condition will often give you a good idea of what you can expect when your property is under their care. If they have children, then you will want to pay attention to how well-behaved they are. The children don't need to be perfect, they are children after all, but there is a big difference between a normal child and one that is willfully destructive. Regardless of how they present themselves during the walkthrough, you will always want to call the previous landlord and ask about the state of the property when the tenant moved out.

The tenant who is loud: Tenants who are excessively noisy can be some of the most frustrating for a landlord to deal. While they are unlikely to cause much damage by themselves, this type of tenant practically ensures that you or your property manager are going to get calls from the neighbors on the regular requesting that you do something about your unruly tenant. If the neighbors skip this step and go right to the police then you may have the authorities requesting that you reign in your tenant as well. This issue is often made all the worse by the fact that when you and the tenant interact they are extremely friendly and always pay the rent on time. Regardless, once the calls start rolling in on the regular you are sure to regret this decision immensely.

What's more, disqualifying a loud tenant can be difficult, regardless of how easy it can be to spot them up front. Signs of a loud tenant include things like stories about rowdy friends, questions about extra outlets for surround sound, questions about the neighbors' attitudes towards parties and similar things are all strong signs that a tenant might make life uncomfortable for you and the neighbors both. Instead, the best way to deal with this potential problem is to point out what the rest of the neighborhood is like and point out that they have your phone number as well. If this doesn't work then you will need to find another reason to legally disqualify them from the property.

The tenant that doesn't pay rent: While dealing with a destructive tenant is never fun, as long as you received their deposit and they pay their rent on time there is little they can do that cannot be undone. That is why the absolute worst type of tenant is the one that uses every excuse under the sun to justify why they are going to be late on the rent and then stretch that timeframe out as long as possible. This is rarely the first time this type of tenant has found themselves "a little short" this month and they have likely learned over time what they can get away with under the law which means they will almost always owe you something.

Luckily, this type of tenant leaves a trail that is typically quite easy to follow as long as you do your homework. This is why it is so important to always run a credit check on every applicant and also get, and verify, their residency history. This is also why you want to have a firm policy in place when it comes to previous evictions as if it has happened before then there is a good chance it could happen again which is more than enough reason to steer clear all on its own.

Sure, sometimes an otherwise good tenant may end up in an untenable situation and have no choice but to go through the eviction process, but when it comes to your first few rental properties you likely won't be able to take that chance which is why sticking to this rule is so important. Always do your due diligence before letting anyone put any money down, you only have yourself to blame by the results if you don't.

The tenant that will have too many animals: While deciding to allow pets in a property is something you will need to consider for yourself, there is a difference between a tenant with one small dog and half a dozen dogs plus as many cats. This is why it is important to have a pet policy in place and do what you can to ensure it is strictly enforced. Unfortunately, this is easier said than done which is why it is important to always check with the previous landlord to see what type of shape the previous property was left in when they vacated. If a previous landlord complains about pets then there is no reason to assume this will not be an issue again in the future. While this may not be enough to disqualify the tenant on its own, it should be enough that you are looking for other reasons to disqualify them.

The lying tenant: The difficulty that a lying tenant will cause is directly proportional to the type of lies they are telling. A tenant that lies about having steady employment but who regularly freelances and can thus pay the rent is one thing, a tenant that lies about being an intravenous drug user is quite another. Unfortunately, even with a tenant who starts off with mild lies, you can often anticipate that they will lie about other things like the state of the property when they moved in or when they move out if it suits them.

Sorting out the liars is one of the more difficult things to do as a landlord as you will have very little information to go off of. This means it is important to pay as close of attention to all the details you do have as possible in order to keep an eye out for anything that might be a bald-faced lie. A lie at this stage should thus be unforgivable as it is the only indication you will get that this type of behavior is something you may have to deal with again in the future.

The party tenant: This is another type of tenant whose tendencies are fine in moderation but intolerable after a certain point. The definition of a tenant that throws a party now and then and one that parties too much is going to vary based on the type of property and where it is located. Too much partying can disrupt the flow of a neighborhood and can lead to drunk and disorderly conduct, fighting, vandalism and more, not to mention illegal behavior of one type or another is virtually guaranteed after a certain point.

Luckily, as long as you don't plan on being too strict, it should be relatively easy to determine right from the start if a tenant is going to fit in with the neighborhood your property is a part of. Checking with their landlord and personal references is a great place to start and this, plus a background check should give you the details you need to determine if they like to take things a bit too much to the extreme for your liking.

The tenant who enjoys too much drama: While most renters want nothing more than to fly under the radar of their landlord until their lease is up, others will only be happy if they are always dealing with some type of issue that needs to be resolved ASAP. These issues usually manifest themselves as a constant barrage of phone calls either following up on a previous issue or informing you about some new emergency. Whatever their favorite reason for calling, you can bet you will be tempted to block their number before everything is said and done.

Weeding out this type of applicant can be difficult at first but is sure to grow easier with a little practice. An easy way to spot this type of tenant is that they are often extremely eager during the walkthrough, taking note of every nook and cranny, especially anything that they feel will have to be fixed before they can move in. They could also be extremely curious about the neighbors and the level of crime in the area. If you feel as though you may be dealing with a dramatic tenant then making it clear that you will not play into their game should be enough to get them to move on.

The tenant that is extremely entitled: A majority of the tenants you deal with over the years will inevitably understand that a tenant/landlord relationship is one of give and take. Now and then, however, you will come across the type of tenants that believe just because they are paying you rent means you are entitled to give them the world in order to make them happy. This is not the tenant that nicely asks that you come out and fix their broken water heater, it is the type of tenant that will insist you come out in the middle of the night because their faucet has sprung a leak. These sorts of tenants will not only make it their mission to make your life miserable from the moment they move in until the day they move out, they will feel it is their right to do so.

Luckily, as long as you are paying attention, this type of tenant is one of the easiest to pick out from the start. Throughout the walkthrough, they are going to be the ones not just pointing out existing issues but demanding that you fix them before they could even begin to move in. They won't have valid things to say about the property either, they will find issue in things that 90 percent of renters would overlook without thinking twice.

The tenant that knows too much: While it may be difficult to disqualify them, you are also going to want to keep an eye out for the type of renter that is overly familiar with the renter laws in your state. Paralegals, lawyers and the like often know just how far they can push things and still stay within in the law. While this will inherently mean that things will never get too out of hand, it will certainly be annoying for the entire length of the lease as they exploit loopholes for personal gain. While this is far from a guarantee, when it comes to your early rentals you want the process to go as smoothly as possible from start to finish.

Writing a lease
Once you have found a tenant that you can deal with, the final thing you will need to consider is the lease that you will write to ensure that your new tenant knows exactly what your expectations are when it comes to the property. It doesn't matter how obvious or outrageous you think specific actions might be, if you don't outline it clearly in your lease then you can expect at least one tenant to eventually try and do it. What's more, as a general rule you can expect tenants to follow rules that are clearly explained upfront and in writing, than they are those that are discussed in person or after they have already moved in. In writing

also ensure that they understand exactly what the consequences for breaking the agreed upon rules will be.

Again, it is of the upmost importance that you have a clear list of consequences when it comes to what will happen if the tenant goes outside your wishes and breaks the rules. More importantly, having everything written down and signed up front will make it easier for you to take appropriate legal action against tenants that do not follow the rules. What follows is a list of recommendations that make for a good starter lease for those who don't have anything specific in mind.

When rent should be paid: It is important to make it clear both what day the rent is due on as well as what the tenant can expect to happen if they are late. Giving the tenant an extra day or so is nice but certainly not required. Likewise, it is important to clearly state what the late fees will be like if the rent is not paid on time. Common options are either a percentage of the rent or a fixed amount for each day the rent is late.

When you are allowed on the property: It is equally important that you make it clear the various reasons and times you may enter the property. Generally speaking, this will be either with justifiable cause or if you give 24-hour warning first.

Disposal of waste: While this shouldn't be necessary, the sad truth is that it is important to make it clear to the tenant that they have to regularly take out their trash and how frequently they must do so. Not only is this a hygiene issue, if your property has too much trash on it then you can be fined be the city which is why it is important to make it clear what you expect in regard to this issue.

The overall state of the property: In order to protect yourself and your property it is important to make it clear that the renter needs to do what they can be reasonably expected to do in order to ensure the property stays in close to the same condition that you found it in. If they fail to do so then you also need to make it clear that you will be keeping their deposit if they don't hold up their end of the bargain. This clause should apply both in the home and on the property in general. You also need to make it clear what will account for natural wear in your opinion to ensure things are as crystal clear as possible.

Pets: Do you allow pets or not? Many of the large apartment complexes owned by real estate investment groups and REITs do not allow pets. They are unwilling to lose the profit it takes to clean an apartment after a pet has been inside. There is also a higher chance for multiple units to be empty at the same time.

If apartment complexes allow pets, the fees are astronomical. A renter may pay as much as $400 for a pet deposit, per pet. They may also be charged with pet rent per month, which can be anywhere from $10 to $100 a month, per pet. A person really has to love their pets to want to pay a high price. There is also an issue of how many pets one can have. Typically, the maximum is two. There are also breed and size restrictions in many apartment complexes. When a person moves out, if the unit needs a deeper cleaning because their pet left an odor or there was damage to doors/walls, then they lose their entire deposit. This is why some apartment complexes have weighed the risk of having pets against the costs they incur and decline to allow pets.

For a person with a single property, trying to rent it, there are other considerations to be made.

1. If a pet damages the carpet, you either need to have it cleaned or rip it out and replace it.
2. If damage occurs to the door trim, doors, window trim, tile, or other flooring due to the pet, you have to fix it.
3. You are usually renting a property in a neighborhood, which may not be happy if a loud animal continually makes noise throughout the day and night.
4. You may lose more than 50% of the possible renters who are looking for a property.

If you decide to allow pets, you should have a strict pet policy that is maintained. For example, if you allow cats and dogs, you should outline how many pets total can be in the property, if there are any breeds you will not allow, and if there are any weight restrictions. The more detailed your pet policy, the easier it will be to bring a renters attention to it when or if it is broken.

You can also ask for a deposit that includes enough to cover cleaning up after pets.

The deposit

Always get a deposit. You can legally request first and last month's rent, as well as a deposit. It will depend on how much the rent is and the area you are trying to rent in. The "last" month's rent can be seen as a deposit too but be clear what can and cannot happen when someone moves out, with regards to the deposit.

Chapter 8: Property Flipping Basics

Fix and flip is the colloquial term for purchasing a less than desirable property, fixing it up, and selling it for a profit. While this can be an extremely time-intensive undertaking if you go it alone, the next few chapters will also discuss putting together a team to ensure the process is as streamlined as possible. While it can be difficult to get started with, if you stick with it in the long-term then you will find that you can make a tidy sum when everything is said and done.

Basics

ARV: When looking for properties that the meet the fix and flip criteria the number one thing you will need to consider for every property is what its After Repair Value (ARV) is. The ARV is the amount that you can expect to sell the property for when everything is said and done and it has been renovated successfully. It is very important to work out the ARV on a property as soon as you find out about it as overestimating this number at the moment could lead to a loss in the long run.

To divine the ARV for a specific property you will need to start with an estimate relating to what you feel you can get the property for out the door. From there, you will want to add in the cost of the renovations, as well as any other costs that will need to be considered while the property is in your hands. An acceptable ARV is no more than 70 of what you believe you can realistically sell the property for in a reasonable period of time. If the property you are considering doesn't meet these standards then you will have no choice but to move on as it is not really worth the effort.

Having a firm ARV in mind needs to be something that you do before you go for the initial property visit as it will ensure you don't get unduly invested in a property that will ultimately go nowhere. While this rule might seem needlessly strict at first, you will find that if you shift it by as much as five percent you start to see serious losses, especially if you end up underestimating the true cost of the renovations.

Think about who will buy the property: When looking at any property and determining the ARV it is also important to take into account the type of person that you expect to purchase it once it is fixed up and on the market. Doing so will make it far easier to decide how much work actually needs to be done as well as what you will likely be able to sell the property for. For example, if you are looking for properties in rural areas then things like extra rooms are important in the outbuildings because the new owners are likely going to want extra space for toys as well as animals. It is also important to know what types of animals the property is zoned for as you can bet someone is bound to ask. Alternately, if you are looking in the suburbs then things like good schools and other family focused amenities bring in premium prices which is why you will want to look at homes with lots of bedrooms and bathrooms.

Regardless of the type of property you are considering, there is money to be made, no matter what the layout may be, as long as you have a clear idea who you are going to try and sell the property to from the start. Focusing on the strengths of the property will not only reduce the need for excessive remodeling, but it will also help you sell the property quickly as well.

Look for added value: When making improvements to a property it is important to keep a very close tally on the value you bring in along the way. It is also a good idea to take pictures with each step as this will but into sharp focus how much work you actually put in as a means of successfully justifying your asking price. This does not mean that you will need to completely renovate the properties that you purchase as you are only going to want to touch the things that are going to directly improve the price of the property as a whole. More specifically, this means you are rarely ever going to want to undertake projects such as enlarging a living room or putting in a completely new kitchen unless the existing rooms are in such poor shape that the property will not sell otherwise. If you want to turn a profit when everything is said and done then keeping the bottom line in the front of your mind should always be your top priority.

When it comes to decorating and design decisions you are going to always want to stick with neutral colors with the exception of pure white. With every choice you make you should be striving to be as inclusive as possible in terms of potential accent styles as you will want as many different people to be able to picture their own possessions in the space as possible.

Everyone who walks in should be able to feel at home in the space and aggressive colors and styles will only limit these possibilities.

Get educated: You cannot locate a cheap house online, purchase the house, and then sell for profit. If it was that easy to flip, everyone in the world would be billionaires. You must be educated before you begin to look at houses. What is it you need to know?

- Understand the ins and outs of your local market. What areas are people buying in right now? What type of house are they buying? Do not look at the new neighborhoods. You want to get the house sold fast.
- Make sure you understand all of your financing options. Are you going to purchase with cash? Are you going to have to get a mortgage loan, or get a home equity line of credit? Make sure that you understand how financing works before you apply for it.
- Have skills when comes to finding good deals. Do research on plumbing, electrician, and landscaping rates. Know the amount it will cost to re-carpet a house. You should know all of this to make sure you find all of the best deals.
- Talk to buyers and do extensive networking before you even start thinking about house flipping. Make sure you do the best you can to build a good relationship with potential buyers. Try having a buyer read when you buy a house; the house will sell when the updates get completed.
- Find a mentor. If you know someone who has successfully flipped houses, ask them to be a

mentor. You could also offer then an incentive for their help. You could give them a percentage of your first profit for their advice and knowledge. They will be more motivated to tutor you and make sure you get a quality education. Offering an incentive will enable you to approach others that you do not know since you are going to be compensating them for their efforts.

Overall renovation tips

Start by breaking every required task down as much as possible: While it can be stressful to think of everything that needs to be done to get a property show ready, especially if you picked it up cheap because it needed a lot of work, you will find that it is helpful to break every task down into its primary components. Not only will this make it easier for you to determine what projects you or your friends and family can take care of without professional help, but it will help make all of those tasks seem more manageable as well.

If you are planning on doing as much of the project yourself as possible, and it is your first time tackling this sort of thing then your best bet is to typically start in the laundry room, where available. The reasons for this are two fold, first, the room is typically on the small side and there likely won't be all that much that needs to be done with the space outside of cleaning and maybe a new coat of paint which means you can use a small success to bolster your confidence moving forward. Even better, if things don't exactly break your way, then you have only botched one of the least important rooms in the house instead of something high value like the bathroom or the kitchen.

Don't overestimate the little things: While they can easily add significant value to a property, many new real estate investors get so focused on the bigger issues that need to be taken care of that they often let the little things go repair. Little things like old outlet covers, dirty fans, old fixtures, chipped doorframes all add up to your detriment, however, which means you are going to want to ensure these things are gone over specifically before you start showing the property.

Chapter 9: Building the Right Team

When you're doing your primary research about how much money you need in order to purchase a property, it's not enough to simply think about the down payment. You're going to want to also consider other factors including taxes, inspection fees, and most importantly the cost of repair. If you're more of the business type and not really the hands-on repairman or repairwoman type, you are more than likely going to have to contract the repairs that you need to get done to other people.

If you have to contract all of the work that needs to be done on the house, you're going to be spending a small fortune on fixing it up and this does not bode well for your profit margin. This is often the reason why handymen will invest their time and energy into flipping property, and this is known in the business as "sweat equity".

If you're someone who is naturally good at putting up drywall, laying tile, and installing products that need to be done by a plumber, then you are going to be saving money on the cost that it would otherwise take to have a professional come in and do this for you. If you don't have the skillset to take on these types of tasks, the next best thing is to develop an arsenal of people who will accomplish these tasks for you on the cheap. Often, if you can guarantee these types of people that you will have consistent work for them to do over a long period of time, they will be more likely to offer you some sort of deal in exchange for their services.

Unfortunately, building the right sort of team can be more difficult than you might hope while also costing more than you likely think you can afford. Luckily, having them in place means that once the property sells successfully you can then pay everyone out while still keeping a decent amount of the profits for yourself. While doing everything yourself will always result in a larger profit, it will also take much longer so that by the time you finish one property by yourself, you and your team could have done three whole projects. This is, of course, assuming you can find team members who are willing to do the work up front, with an understanding of what the payment arrangement is going to be.

Assuming you don't have the funds to front the renovation costs up front, this is going to be the first thing you are going to want to consider. Once more, a local real estate investment club in an invaluable resource in this scenario as members can often point you in the right direction. A personal referral also means you know that you can count on work being done on time and to the standard of quality you would hope for, especially when compared to the hit or miss nature of online referrals.

Support staff: While a traditional real estate agent will likely be willing to work with you when it comes to finding the types of properties that you are looking for; for a small cut of course, for the best results, you are going to want to seek out an independent REO real estate agent. An REO agent is different from a more traditional real estate agent in that they specialize in homes that are in bank foreclosure. While finding an REO agent will likely take a bit longer, the end result will be more than worth the extra effort as you will have access to a far superior range of properties as a whole. Real estate agents who are known to specialize in short sales are also worth keeping an eye out for. These individuals are much rarer than traditional real estate agents but all the work you will likely do tracking them down and building a positive relationship will be returned 10 fold in the quality types of properties they will provide you access to.

The next two people you will need to find for your team are going to be a certified public account who specializes in real estate and an attorney who does the same. While these folks are sure to charge a fair amount for their services, in this instance you will very much get what you pay for. If the time comes and you ever need their services in more than a superficial way you will be extremely happy to have them in your corner. Looking for a local recommendation from a real estate club or a trusted mentor is recommended but keep in mind their fees are likely not as fixed as they may like you to think so there is often a little wiggle room if you ask nicely.

While a real estate lawyer shouldn't be hard to find, locating a CPA with real estate experience might be trickier, especially in smaller towns. Perseverance is important in this instance, however, as the tax code can easily be interpreted in a wide variety of different ways which means that there is often an interpretation that works out in your favor, if only you know the person to find it for you. it is also important to ensure your lawyer and your CPA work well together as they will hopefully be seeing each other regularly. You will want them both to make sure your business plan for each new property is up to snuff as well.

Contractor: Once you have a quality support team in place, you can move on to the person you will be working most closely with on your flipping venture, your contractor. While you may be able to handle smaller projects on your own, assuming you are relatively handy that is, on anything larger you will be far better served by letting the professionals handle it as what you pay in additional expenses you will be able to more than make up for with the increased rate you will be able to get your properties to market. This is why it is important to choose not just one contractor, but two in case the first does not work out.

The reason the general contractor is so important is that they are the one who essentially runs the project. They will often come with their own team of subcontractors as well who you will be free to use or dismiss as you see fit. Finding a good contractor does require some legwork, however, which is why it is recommended that you follow the steps outlined below for the best results.

1. The first step to successfully finding a subcontractor involves finding recommendations. If you don't have a local real estate club to ask about such things then you will want to check with local real estate agents to see who they use. Along similar lines,

building inspectors are another good source of information as they are sure to remember the names of the people who have worked on the best projects they've seen. What's more, building relationships with both of these types of folks is almost sure to pay off somewhere down the line. Finally, stopping at local lumber mills and asking after contractors that always buy the highest-quality products will often generate some leads as well.

2. After you have your starter list of names, the next thing you are going to want to do is to conduct a round of phone interviews in order to save yourself from having to meet face to face with those contractors who obviously aren't going to work out. Important questions to ask during the interview include things such as:
    • What type of projects are they comfortable with?
    • How many projects do they work on at once?
    • Would they be able to wait for payment until the property sells?
    • Are they able to provide references?

3. With that out of the way, you will then want to meet with the best candidates and get to know then a little better as you will be spending a fair amount of time with them moving forward. You will also want to discuss your future plans in detail, as well as get a general estimate for the job on any properties you currently have

your eye on, just for reference.

4. Finally, you will want to follow up on the references for any of the candidates that managed to make it this far. This is one of the most important steps in the process as you are putting a lot of trust in this person and need to know that they are going to follow through with their side of the bargain.

Subcontractors: Even though your general contractor trusts the chosen subcontractors, that does not mean that you have to trust them, too. It is a good idea to get to know your subcontractors before they begin working on your home. Ask for samples of their work and find out from your contractor why he or she likes them so much. If there is something that you do not like, consider trying to find other ones. Your general contractor will likely have contacts with other people who will be able to help you find subcontractors who are just perfect for your investment property.

All subcontractors should have samples of the work that they have done. They should be willing to show them to you. It is a good idea to do a quick check of their credentials before you make the decision to allow your general contractor to hire them to work on your project. You never know what may be lurking under the surface of what seems like a great business. Make sure that they are efficient at what they do, too. You don't want your entire project to be held up because your plumber doesn't even know how to install a new commode.

Something that you may not know is that you can hire your general contractor without accepting the work of his or her chosen subcontractors. You need to be happy with all of the work that is being done on your home and if the subcontractors are not providing that to you, feel free to fire them and replace them with a company that you like better. Just because the general contractor that you have hired likes a certain company does not mean that you will need to use that company for your project. Your general contractor should understand that you would prefer to use someone that you like better.

Chapter 10: Selling the Property

Marketing: Marketing has changed in recent years. In fact, ever since the internet became a public entity, the real estate world changed. Real estate gurus had the idea of starting various sites that post available listings, which makes your work slightly easier. Clients can look online at listings and then contact the listing agent to inquire about the property. It can also make things a little harder because the listing agent is the name that appears on the MLS details.

The listing agent can be contacted directly, so that cuts out the need for two agents to be part of the deal. Although certain things have become a little difficult, other aspects of marketing have become somewhat easier.

Here are avenues you should explore for marketing:
- Social media, including LinkedIn, Facebook, Twitter
- Real Estate Websites: Realtor.com, Zillow.com, etc.
- Creating your own website
- Putting a page on the business website (if you house your office in another real estate office)
- Business cards
- Joining real estate investment groups/clubs
- Real Estate seminars
- Renovation (fix and flip) seminars
- Blogging on WordPress.com
- Writing or having a real estate book written for Kindle

These suggestions are going to help you get your name out there. You still market in old fashioned means, such as phone books, newspapers, and other similar media. However, you want to make sure the bulk of your marketing is through networking resources and online resources. Utilizing these avenues will give you a chance to access more people, gain referrals, and make your business more successful.

It will still take time for the first sale to happen, but at least you are doing all that you can with networking and marketing for real estate sales. Your reputation in the business is going to matter. Make sure you keep your integrity, not only among clients, but among others in the same business as well.

Ensure the house is in the best shape possible
First and foremost, it is going to be likely that the sellers of the property are going to look to you to tell them what they need to do in order to get their property into the best shape possible. Consider making them a checklist with the following listed on it.

Timing your Open House: Open houses are best on Friday, Saturday, and Sunday. This gives one weekday for a person to see the house if they work weekends. Weekends are when most people are free, but not all. Another option if you work in a neighborhood that has many people working weekends, is to stage an evening open house. You can catch them after work any day of the week.

Make sure you are not hosting an open house when there is a festival, sports game, big concert, or other big events that would draw your potential buyers away. Most people need a house, but they are more apt to choose an event that is not recurring versus an open house that could be scheduled on a different day.

Start with a good first impression: The first impression that a property offers can literally make or break a sale in the first 30 seconds. It is important to stress this to sellers as a way to get them to freshen up things like the exterior paint or landscaping. Ensure they include an easy to see address, remove vehicles from the driveway and clean and remove all clutter as well.

Hire professional cleaners: No matter how motivated a seller is, odds are a professional is going to get things cleaner than they ever could. While some sellers will balk at the cost, it is important to stress how important a spic and span property is its overall appeal during the showing.

Less is more: If the property that you have been enlisted to help sell is absolutely full of things like furniture or knickknacks, then it will be in your best interest to convince the seller to move some of the clutter to another location to give the property a chance to breath. The goal should be for the property to not look barren, but to be on the minimalist side of the spectrum without a doubt. The same goes for wall or floor coverings, potential buyers like to see what they are getting. Keep accent pieces, and mirrors on the walls to open up closed spaces but keep it simple.

Making a good impression: before anyone enters your home, they are going to see the front door, any front yard, and the exterior of the home. The exterior door should be painted, if there are any chips, scratches, or peeling paint issues. Your client will need to freshen up the landscaping, and cover over the main bruises on the exterior paint. The garage door, if there is one, needs to be cleaned if not repainted. A new mailbox or a painted one needs to welcome potential buyers.

Remove personal items: personal items will take away from the potential buyer's sight. They will see family photos and other personal items that detract from the potential of the house. What they want to see is a mantle over the fireplace that is empty, where they can envision their own pictures. They also want to see a clean fridge, where they know there is no dirt, dent, or personal images.

Lock pets in a specific area: if your client has pets make certain the pets are out of the way. It is best to have the animals out of the house, but if there is no option, then they should be in an unimportant room. If at all possible, the pets should be outside or taken with the client for the time the open house will be ongoing. This way potential buyers can open doors, without worry that a pet will escape or be locked in a closet.

Set up signs: You will want to have signs up on the main street, at any turn the potential buyer needs to make, and at the house. The more signs that are visible the easier it will be to get people into the house.

Advertising: How do you advertise real estate? You cannot rely on a sign in the front yard of a property. There must be other ways that you can generate sales and gain potential clients.

- Social Media: Social media is not only a way to get your listings out there and network, but it is also a way for you to advertise. Create ads that provide an advertisement of your skills, as well as profile pages that tell people about yourself.

- YouTube Videos: Videos work in targeting select clientele. Investors are often looking for video tutorials and potential property to purchase. Sellers need tips on how to stage their home. Buyers want a virtual walk through of a home. Videos are a perfect way to give everyone what they want. Make the video funny, insightful, and educational. It should be no more than a minute, whether it advertises a listing, who you are, or your business.

- Write Effective Ad Copy: If you are not a writer, hire one. You need a writer who can create listings that sell properties. You also need a writer who can create ad copy. It is important to tell a story about a property to appeal to the buyer's emotions, as well as providing the reader with the facts.

Chapter 11: Property Wholesaling

If you are interested in the active investment nature of property flipping but don't want to have to worry about the part in the middle when renovations are actually done before making a profit, then property wholesaling may be the real estate investment strategy for you. The basic property wholesale transaction proceeds thusly, first, you find a property that you know could be flipped for a profit, next you negotiate the price of the property to a point that you and another investor can both make money on it and then you sell the property for a profit.

Before you go out trawling for properties to wholesale, you will need to keep in mind what your particular state has to say about wholesaling as different states see it differently and have different laws in place to regulate the practice. The laws you are going to want to definitely check into relate to how your state feels about brokering. Generally speaking, as the person who found the buyer and the seller of a given property transaction that would make you the broker in this situation. If your state considers you a broker for wholesaling, then you are going to need to find out if brokers in your state are required to have real estate licenses, as many do. If your state considers wholesaling a form of assigning a contract, then it is unlikely that you will be required to have a real estate license to do so. Regardless, the best course of action is to simply schedule some time with a real estate lawyer who can set you straight.

If you live in a state that does require you to get your real estate license in order to officially wholesale properties, you can either proceed down that route which will have multiple ancillary benefits for your real estate investment career, or if you are anxious to get started, you can instead perform essentially the same process via what is known as a double close. To perform a double close, you are going to need two willing individuals, the original seller and the ultimate buyer, to work with you in tandem to ensure things are done in a legal fashion. To start, you and the primary seller agree to a contract and wait for the deal to close, meanwhile, you then stagger a second deal with the ultimate buyer, agree to a contract, and wait for that deal to close a few days after the first. You then use the funds from the second transaction to pay for the first.

Ensuring that this type of double deal is possible often comes down to the type of contract that the primary seller is willing to enter into with you and any issues they are currently abiding by relating to encumbrance. Encumbrance is any one of several types of claims that limits how the property can be transferred while also limiting its free use until the encumbrance related issue has been dealt with. The various types of easements that you may have to deal with when wholesaling properties are outlined below.

Easement: An easement can either be used to allow another person to improve a property that they do not own, or it can be used to prevent the owner of a property from improving it in specific ways. If you come across this type of encumbrance you are going to need to see it resolved before most flippers will even touch it in case the easement prevents them from making the changes they need to if they want to make a profit on the property. Additionally, depending on the type of property that you are dealing with, you may need to negotiate easement rights that do not come along with the original contract. If, for example, you purchase a property which draws its water from a well located on another person's property based on an easement that is already in place then the water rights would not, necessarily, transfer along with the property itself.

Encroachment: An encroachment easement relates to instances such as property lines disputes which can lead to secondary issues like issues with trespassing or nuisance in regard to what were assumed to be pre-existing usage rights. If left unresolved this can lead to encumbrance being placed on the property until the issue is resolved.

Lease: If you are planning to purchase a property that currently has some type of lease on it then you will be encumbered until that lease is up unless you are able to work out some agreement with the tenant or transfer the agreement to the lease along with the title of the property.

Lien: If you are looking at property that has a lien associated with the title then this means the previous owner either defaulted on a loan or used the land as collateral in another loan that was then defaulted on. This means the creditor is allowed to sell their land as a way of recouping their losses. A lien can also be placed on a piece of property by the government if the previous own owed unpaid taxes. Finally, a lien can be placed on a property if serious work was done to the property that was not paid for and the judge rules in favor of the person who did the work.

Making an offer
Once you have a property in your sites, the next step will be to determine what is known as the maximum allowable offer which is the most you can pay for the property while still turning a profit. This amount can be found by taking the ARV and subtracting out what the person buying the property from you is going to expect to make on it. From there you will also want to subtract out the renovations costs, as well as any other costs. Finally, you will need to decide what you need to make the transaction and from there you will end up with your maximum allowable offer.

While the easiest way to come up with accurate estimate for each of these numbers is going to be experience, plain and simple, finding a general contractor who is willing to visit properties and help you estimate the potential cost of repairs is a good place to start as if you pay attention you should be able to get the basics down relatively easily. As always, a local real estate club is a good place to start looking for this type of person.

If this does not appear to be an option, you can also research the potential ARV of given properties in an area based on the list of criteria that you devise, though it often takes more time to get up and running using this method. You could also start by befriending a real estate agent and shadowing them to determine the ARV of the properties they work with. Finding an agreeable real estate agent should be easy with a few tries, you will also find another outlet to search for new and potentially profitable properties. Don't forget, the importance of a good team cannot be overstated.

Maximizing the contract's potential: Once you have a signed contract ready to go, one of the last things you need to do is to find a seller that you know will purchase the property for a price that you will be able to turn a profit on. There are a variety of buyer types you can choose from, though ideally, you will want to locate a cash buyer. A cash buyer is a real estate investor who has collected enough funds to ensure they have cash on hand for any properties they want to purchase. In fact, a majority of the more successful property flippers you meet are likely to fall into this category. Cash buyers are ideal because they will allow you to transfer the contract and walk away with your earnings on the same day.

While you might not think that there are lots of folks out there with $100,000 or more burning a whole in their pockets, the fact of the matter is that if you have done your job up to this point and managed to get the property for a price you can profit from then you should be able to find someone who will take it off your hands. As you might expect, the best place to find these types of individuals will be at a local real estate investment club and if no one in the club fits the bill then they can likely point you in the right direction.

Once you have a small stable of cash buyers on hand you very likely won't need to find any more as three or four could very well be enough to set you up for life.

You can develop a mutually beneficial relationship with these individuals if you play your cards right and establish working relationships that last decades. With this out of the way, all you need to do is take your share of the profits and be on your way. Many property wholesalers falter at this point, however, because they get greedy and try and upsell their properties an excessive amount. This is shortsighted, however, as the benefits of being reasonable far outweigh the extra profit you will make in the short-term.

Chapter 12: REITs

If you are interested in the idea of investing in real estate but don't like the idea of dealing with the trouble of finding a rental property to purchase, then investing in Real Estate Investment Trusts (REITs) might be more your speed. With this passive income stream, you don't need to worry about having lots of cash already on hand for a large down payment and can get started with virtually any amount. This is because when you invest in REITs you are investing in individual shares the same way you would as if you were investing in a company via buying into their stock. This means, instead of worrying if a given property is ultimately going to turn a profit, all you need to do is choose a REIT that has a proven track record and let their team of analysts make profitable decisions for you. In return for your investment, you will receive dividends just as you would if you invested in dividend producing stocks.

Investing in REITs does have its own drawbacks, however, as it typically requires you to pay taxes on the dividends you receive in addition to paying taxes on the income used to purchase your shares in the first place. If you are hoping to generate passive income as a retirement strategy, however, then you can negate this double taxation by putting the money into an IRA account and agreeing not to touch the funds until you are ready to retire.

REITs were created in the 1960s as a way for the average working individual to partake in the profits generated by larger real estate investments such as hotels and major office complexes, to that end they are required to ensure that 90 percent of their profits return to the shareholders and that more than five individuals control 50 percent of the available shares. Additionally, if you don't approve of the current direction of the REIT then you are free to get rid of your shares freely on the open market at any time without taking any type of penalty. Share prices fluctuate just like stock prices do so you can make the right choice for you at any time.

Choosing a REIT: When it comes time to choose the REIT that is right for you, the first thing you are going to want to do is plenty of research. Luckily, as you will soon see most REITs are pretty self-explanatory when it comes to their holdings which means you can often go and visit them yourself in order to see if everything appears to be on the up and up. Additionally, you will be able to look up their historical dividend yields, with 7 percent being the goal to shoot for. You will also want to consider the amount of growth it has seen for the past few years which can be determined by looking into their net income and operation funds from which you can determine their year over year cash flow. You are going to want to choose a REIT that has at least a 5 percent average growth range per year.

Another useful statistic to track is the number of the REIT's shareholders are institutional investors. Institutional investors include things like investment firms and other professional investment organizations which means that the more institutional investors a REIT has, the greater the odds that it is going to perform as anticipated. Last but not least, when it comes time to price out individual shares, you are going to want to focus on REITs that are in your budget, but at the same time are not budget priced. Shares that are priced to move are a sure indication that the REIT that is offering them has either just been through some rough times or that it expects rough times ahead, and either way it is a proposition that you should want no part of.

Equity REITs
Equity REITs are those which are actively engaged in acquiring, managing, renovating and selling real estate. This is the most profitable types of REITs as a rule, which makes the most common REIT and the most successful. Equity REITs typically focus on a specific type of real estate including resorts and hotels, storage facilities, health care facilities, office facilities, industrial facilities, retail facilities or residential facilities, all of which have different strengths and weaknesses depending on local markets.

As such, if you are planning on investing in one of these types of REITs it is best to do some homework beforehand and determine just what the market is like for the type of real estate in question:

Residential: One of the most common types of REITs is the residential variety that typically deals in condominiums and apartment buildings. You will know if this type of REIT is a good investment if the amount of demand exceeds the supply. If there are lots of new apartment buildings in the area of the REIT's holdings, it might be better to keep looking at additional options.

Retail: REITs that focus on retail are typically further specialized into either shopping malls or shopping centers. The types of properties that these REITs focus on are quite expensive to build which means there will rarely be more space available than the demand calls for. Nevertheless, it is easy to see how successful these REITs are doing, simply visit their holdings and determine for yourself if the complexes or shopping malls are in a period of boom or bust.

Offices and industrial parks: This type of possible REIT candidates are typically subject to longer lease periods which means their profitability is largely tied to how the market was doing when the space was initially rented last. This can go either way for the REIT as a period of low rents can curtail profits for years to come while higher rents will keep things looking up despite the occasional vacancy. To determine what part of the cycle the holdings in question are in you can call properties in the area and check rental rates against long term averages.

Storage: When it comes to jumping on the REIT bandwagon, there is no cheaper way to do so than via a REIT that focuses on storage units. Storage unit use has been rising steadily in the United States for the past 20 years and this type of REIT has proven itself to be reliable and quite resistant to downturns as well. As long as there are not too many competing services in a given area, this type of REIT is almost always going to generate slow and steady profits.

Hotels and resorts: Investing in these REITs is typically on the high end of the cost spectrum and is often one of the riskier propositions as it is closely tied to the general success of the worldwide markets because people simply take fewer vacations when the economy is weak. As such, if you are planning in investing in this type of REIT you will need to be fairly confident in the market in general.

Non-equity REITs

Mortgage REITs: These types of REITs are those that are instead interested in holding, acquiring and underwriting the debt associated with real estate purchases. Buying shares in these REITs are closer to owning a debt portfolio than owning a portion of a physical asset.

Hybrid REITs: For those who simply cannot make up their minds, a hybrid REIT offers investment opportunities for both mortgage loan and equity property investment. While not as common as regular equity REITs, they are a good choice for those looking to diversify as much as possible all in one place.

REIT tips to keep in mind

- Your investment in a REIT is liquid versus other real estate deals.
- You need to assess the growth in earnings, which is made from high occupancy and increasing rents, as well as assess the lower costs and potential new business opportunities.
- Research the management team because it is the team that will decide if a facility is upgraded if more facilities/services are offered, and help to increase the demand for the property.

- You do need to be cautious about wage growth. Wage growth directly effects whether rent can increase. Rent increases can reduce potential renters, even make it impossible for renters to stay in the property they have been renting for years. There is a fine line between increasing rent to make a higher profit and ensuring that the property stays rented. The management team has to know the best option in the rental market to ensure they do not turn away potential income for a thought of gaining higher earnings.

Conclusion

Thanks for making it through to the end of *Real Estate Investing: How To Make Your Riches From Rental Properties and Flipping Houses, And Build Passive Income By Mastering The Property Investment Game*, let's hope it was informative and able to provide you with all of the tools you need to achieve your goals, whatever it is that they may be. Just because you've finished this book doesn't mean there is nothing left to learn on the topic, and expanding your horizons is the only way to find the mastery you seek.

While, generally speaking, the steps to success with real estate investment are relatively straightforward, it is important to not get ahead of yourself early on in the process. While eventually, you will have the network of contacts, leads on upcoming properties and experience finding the best deals, that all comes with time and it is important to manage your expectations accordingly. While it is certainly important to set goals if you hope to be successful in real estate, it is also important that those goals are realistic if you want them to motivate you towards success as opposed to holding you back with unrealistic demands.

All told it may take several months before you have done enough research to find the perfect neighborhood and then several months more before you find the perfect property. While your individual time to profit might be shorter, it is important to keep in mind how long the process might realistically take so that you can be prepared. Just remember, investing in real estate is a marathon, not a sprint which means that slow and steady wins the race.

Finally, if you found this book useful in anyway, a review on Amazon is always appreciated!

Description

Regardless if you are looking to start investing for the first time or are looking to enhance an existing investment portfolio, real estate is an ideal choice. Ideal, that is, if you choose wisely, but the complex ins and outs of the various types of real estate investment make doing so far from a sure thing. If you are interested in ensuring you make the right decisions, then *Real Estate Investing: How To Make Your Riches From Rental Properties and Flipping Houses, And Build Passive Income By Mastering The Property Investment Game* is the book you have been waitin gfor.

Inside you will find everything you need in order to help make the process more straight forward, started with real estate investment successfully starting with the basics including useful investment lingo, how to decide if real estate if real estate is right for you and additional starter tips to help you get started on the right foot. Next, you will learn essentials when it comes to paying for property, finding the ideal property and negotiating the deal when the time comes.

From there you will learn about a wide variety of different real estate investment opportunities including rental property of the traditional and turn key variety as well as the responsibilities that come with being a landlord. You will then learn the ins and out of property flipping including determining when a property is a good deal and building a fix and flip team. Finally, you will learn the basics of property wholesaling and REITs as well.

So, what are you waiting for? Take control of your financial future like never before and buy this book today!

www.ingramcontent.com/pod-product-compliance
Lightning Source LLC
Chambersburg PA
CBHW050531190326
41458CB00007B/1733

.